Jack and the Baked Beanstalk

A play by David Wood

Illustrated by Chantal Stewart

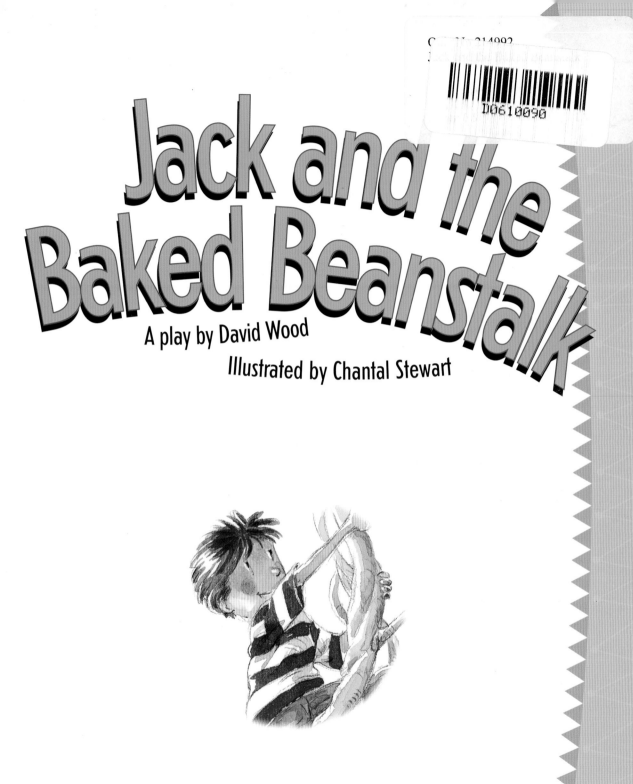

Characters

Jack

Mother

Giant

Buttercup

Stallholder

Cue Card Holder

Sound FX Helpers

Audience

Turn to page 29 for Sound and Stage Tips

Jack and the Baked Beanstalk

Scene 1   Outside the Cottage

(Buttercup walks onstage.)

Buttercup: *(Greeting the Audience.)* Mooooooo!

(Enter Mother.)

Mother: Buttercup, now stop that mooing!
Where's my Jack and what's he doing?

Buttercup: *(As if to say 'I don't know'.)* Moo-oo-oo!

Mother: What? You don't know?
Look, we've got visitors.
(To Audience.) Hello!
(Cue Card Holder holds up the cue card.)

Audience: Hello!

Mother: I'm tickled pink you're here today.
You're just in time to see our play.
Now, I'm the merry Mrs Mac,
This is Buttercup, this is Jack.

Buttercup: *(As if to say 'He's not here'.)* Moo-oo-oo!

Mother: Jack! Where's he gone, my lazy son?
Have you seen him, anyone?
(Cue Card Holder holds up the cue card.)

Audience: No!

Mother: Call him, would you? Shout out 'Jack!'
Make him hear and hurry back.
(Cue Card Holder holds up the cue card.)

Mother and Audience:	Jack!
Mother:	Louder!
Mother and Audience:	Jack!

(Enter Jack.)

Jack:	Here I am, Mum. Sorry I'm late!
Mother:	Listen Jack! I'm in such a state.
Jack:	I'm hungry Mum, I want my tea.
Buttercup:	*(As if to say 'So do I'.)* Moo-oo-oo!
Jack:	And so does she.
Mother:	I'm sorry son, it isn't funny. We've got no food, we've got no money. We've reached rock bottom Jack, so now I think we'll have to sell the cow.
Buttercup:	*(sadly)* Moo!

Jack: Buttercup? Oh, please Mum, no!

Mother: Sorry, but she'll have to go.
Wend your way to market Jack.
Take the cow—don't bring her back.

Jack: But Buttercup is like a pet!

Mother: Ask for the best price you can get.

Jack: But …

Mother: That's enough! My mind's made up.

Jack: Right Mum. Come on Buttercup!

Buttercup: *(angrily)* Moo!

Jack: Come on!

Buttercup: *(struggling)* Moo!

Jack: Ooooo!

(All exit.)

Scene 2   The Market

(The Stallholder is at his stall. Enter Jack and Buttercup.)

Jack: Cow for sale, roll up, roll up!
             Who will buy my Buttercup?

Stallholder: Special offer, don't be shy!
             Give my magic beans a try!

             (He shows Jack some baked beans cans.)

Jack: Magic beans? I don't believe you.

Stallholder:	Listen lad, would I deceive you?
	Plant them and before your eyes,
	I guarantee a big surprise.
	Like some?

| Jack: | Yes, but … |

| Stallholder: | Good, how many? |

| Jack: | Sir, I haven't got a penny. |
| | Come on, Buttercup … |

Stallholder:	No lad, stop!
	No need to pay, we'll do a swap.
	The cow for me, the beans for you.

Jack:	*(To Audience.)* Er … yes or no,
	What should I do?
	(He encourages the Audience to advise him.)
	All right sir, thank you, I agree.
	The cow for you, the beans for me.

Stallholder: Here you are, lad.

(*Gives Jack the baked beans cans.*)

Jack: Thank you sir.
Take the cow, look after her.

Buttercup: (*sadly*) Moo!

Jack: Goodbye Buttercup. Don't be sad.
Goodbye sir.

Stallholder: Goodbye lad.

(*All exit.*)

Scene 3   Outside the Cottage

(Mother enters, followed by Jack.)

Jack: Hello Mum. It's me, I'm back!

Mother: That was speedy. Well done Jack!
          So did you sell the cow?

Jack: Oh yes.
          And listen Mum, you'll never guess …

Mother: Jack, don't keep me in suspense.
          Where's the cash, the pounds and pence?
          Tell me quickly what you got.

Jack: I got these beans Mum.

Mother: You got what?

Jack: These beans, you see … they're magic Mum.

Mother: Are you joking Jack, or just plain dumb?

Jack: I tell you Mum, these beans *are* magic.

Mother: I tell you Jack, I think it's tragic.
Tragic that our cow is lost
And these baked beans were all she cost.
Next, I s'pose, you nincompoop,
You'll sell your mum for a can of soup!

Jack: But Mum …

Mother: How dare you answer back!
          You deserve a smack, Jack Mac.
          You've brought me misery and gloom.
          Get inside! Go to your room!

          (She chases him offstage.)

Jack: *(offstage)* All right Mum. No need to shout!

Mother: *(offstage)* Give me those cans.
          I'll throw them out!

Jack: *(offstage)* But Mum, they're magic.
Listen, do!

Mother: *(offstage)* Quiet, or I'll throw you out too!

(The beans cans are thrown onto the stage.)

Sound FX: *(A noise like a drum beat, to accompany the landing of each can on the stage.)*

Jack: *(offstage)* But Mum …

Mother: *(offstage)* Jack, that's your final warning.
Not another word till morning.

Sound FX: *(Night-time noises or music. The beanstalk slowly grows. Growing, stretching noises.)*

Scene 4   The Beanstalk

(Jack walks onstage and suddenly sees the tall beanstalk.)

Jack: Hey, look what's grown up in the night!
A baked bean tree, the man was right!
The beans were magic, they grew like seeds.
I'll find out where the beanstalk leads.

Sound FX: *(Exciting music as Jack mimes climbing the beanstalk.)*

*(Two legs of the Giant's bed can be seen in the clouds.
Jack appears.)*

Jack: I've climbed so high my ears went pop!
I'm in the clouds! I've reached the top!
Phew! I think I need a rest.
It's cold. I wish I'd worn a vest.
Hey look, what's this? A funny tree?
No, it's a bed—too big for me.
The biggest bed I ever saw!

Giant: *(Offstage snoring sounds.)* ZZzzzzzzzzzzzz

Jack: What's that?

Giant: *(Offstage snoring sounds.)* ZZzzzzzzzzzzzz

Jack: A giant snore!
A giant snore must mean that on this bed
A snoring giant rests his head!

Giant: *(Offstage very loud snoring sounds.)* ZZZZZZZZZ

Jack: Courage, Jack. He's fast asleep.
Why not take a little peep?

Giant: (*Offstage stretching and yawning sounds.*)

Yaaah! Ooooh! Yaaah!

(*Suddenly a giant foot appears.*)

Jack: Look, a foot! All dirty pink!

Pooh, it pongs. Boy, what a stink!

Listen, for a bit of fun,

Shall I tickle it, everyone?

(*Cue Card Holder holds up the cue card.*)

Audience: Yes!

Jack: *(Tickling foot.)* Tickle! Tickle!

Giant: *(offstage)* Ho, ho, ho!

Jack: *(Tickling foot again.)* Tickle!

Giant: *(offstage)* Stop it! No, no, no!
Fee, fi, fo, fum!

Jack: He's woken up! I want my mum!

Giant: *(offstage)* Fee, fi, fo, fum!
         I smell breakfast, here I come!

Jack: Breakfast?

         (The foot traps Jack.)

Giant: *(offstage)* Gotcha!

Jack: Don't eat me, please!
         I'm tough! And I've got knobbly knees!

Giant: *(offstage)* You've no idea how much this means.
For years my only food's been beans.
Baked beans—canned, not even fresh.
Now I fancy human flesh!

Jack: You monstrous giant, I'm not your snack!

(Jack wriggles free.)

Giant: *(offstage)* Come back! Come back!

Sound FX: *(A tinkling noise to accompany the landing of four giant gold coins thrown from offstage.)*

Giant: *(offstage)* Take that! *(Coin lands.)* And that! *(Coin lands.)* And that! *(Coin lands.)* And that! *(Coin lands.)* I'm running out of ammo! Drat!

Jack: Sorry Giant, you scored a duck. And look, I can't believe my luck! Every coin he threw at me Is solid gold, as you can see!

Giant: *(offstage)* Where's my breakfast? Fee, fi, fo …

Jack: I think it's time for me to go!

(Carrying some coins, Jack mimes climbing down the beanstalk.)

Scene 6   Outside the Cottage

(Enter Mother carrying two giant gold coins.)

Mother: Jack, Jack, what's going on?
When I woke up, I found you gone.
And then I got an awful fright—
This thing had sprung up overnight!
And then these gold coins hurtled down
And very nearly broke my crown!

Jack: You see, the beans *were* magic, Mum …

Giant: *(offstage)* Fee, fi, fo, fum!

Mother: What's all that
         Fee, fi, fo, fumming?

Jack: Look out Mum, the giant's coming!

         (A large boot appears.)

Mother: Look at that, Jack! What a whopper!

Jack: Quick Mum, hide! I'll get the chopper!

         (Mother hides. Jack exits.)

Giant:	*(offstage)* Where's my breakfast? Where's my prize?
	(Jack returns with a fake axe.)
Jack:	I'll cut this giant down to size!
Sound FX:	*(Chop! Chop! Chop! Chop!)*
Jack:	Here he goes!
Sound FX:	*(Creaking noises to suggest the beanstalk beginning to fall. The boot disappears.)*
Giant:	*(offstage)* No, mercy, stop! Aaaaaah!
Sound FX:	*(A loud crash, tinkle, tinkle!)*
Jack:	That crash must mean The giant is now an old has-been.

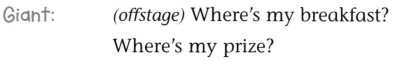

Mother:	*(emerging)* What's happened son?
Jack:	The giant is dead!
	We're safe, we've won!
Mother:	Good riddance to that fat gorilla!
	Three cheers for Jack the Giant Killer!
	(Mother encourages the Audience to join in.
	Cue Card Holder holds up the cue card.)
Mother and Audience:	Hip, hip, hooray!
	Hip, hip, hooray!
Mother:	Hip, hip, hooray! Oh, happy day!

Jack: And with this gold we're rich forever.

Mother: I always said my Jack was clever!
           But son, there's one thing left to do.
           I miss the sound of Buttercup's moo.
           If only we could work out how
           We might get back our dear old cow.

Jack: The magic of the beans, maybe,
           Will help us one more time. Let's see!
           (To Audience.) Everyone say after me,
           Abracadabra, riddle me ree!

Audience: Abracadabra, riddle me ree!

Jack:	Bring back Buttercup, after three!
	(Cue Card Holder holds up the cue card.)
Jack and Audience:	One! Two! Three!
Sound FX:	*(Whooshing noise to suggest magic.)*
	(Enter Buttercup.)
Buttercup:	*(happily)* Moo!
Mother and Jack:	We've done it! Look, she's back! Goodbye from Buttercup, Mum and Jack!
Buttercup:	*(As if to say goodbye.)* Moo-oo!

Sound and Stage Tips

About This Play

This play is a story you can read with your friends in a group or act out in front of an audience. Before you start reading, choose a part or parts you would like to read or act.

There are five main parts in this play, so make sure you have readers for all the parts. You will also need to have at least two Sound FX Helpers and one Cue Card Holder to help move the props, make the sound effects and hold up the cue cards. As the Giant is offstage throughout the play, it is important that his voice sounds loud and clear.

Reading the Play

It's a good idea to read the play through to yourself before you read it as part of a group. It is best to have your own book, as that will help you too. As you read the play through, think about each character and how they might look and sound. How are they behaving? What sort of voice might they have?

Rehearsing the Play

Rehearse the play a few times before you perform it for others. It is important for the readers to practise listening for the sound effects and matching them to the actions, such as climbing the beanstalk.

Remember you are an actor as well as a reader. Your facial expressions and the way you move your body will really help the play to come alive!

Using Your Voice

Remember to speak out clearly and be careful not to read too quickly! Speak more slowly than you do when you're speaking to your friends.

Keep in mind that the audience is hearing your words for the first time.

For *Jack and the Baked Beanstalk*, it is important that the readers practise saying the rhyming lines.

Remember to look at the audience and at the other actors, making sure everyone can hear what you are saying.

Creating Sound Effects (FX)

Sound effects are an important part of this play. The Sound FX Helpers can create atmosphere by making sounds to match the action, such as Jack climbing up and down the beanstalk, the beans growing, the Giant stomping and Buttercup's magical return. See if there are any other places where sounds could be used.

Sets and Props

Once you have read the play, make a list of the things you will need. Here are some ideas to help your performance. You may like to add some of your own.

- Cottage cut-out
- Market stall
- Baked beans cans (made from cardboard or fabric)
- Beanstalk
- Cowbell and lead for Buttercup
- Drums
- Two legs for Giant's bed
- Cloud cut-outs
- Giant's foot
- Fake gold coins
- Fake axe

- Large boot
- Cue cards: 'Hello!', 'No!', 'Jack!', 'Yes!', 'Hip, hip, hooray!' and '1, 2, 3'

Costumes

This play can be performed with or without costumes. If you wish to dress up, you may find the following useful.

- Dress, shawl and headscarf for Mother
- Jeans and T-shirt for Jack
- Hat and vest for the Stallholder
- Brown hessian sack, ears and tail for Buttercup

Have fun!

 Ideas for guided reading

Learning objectives: prepare, read and perform playscripts, compare organisation of scripts with stories; identifying the use of powerful verbs; take different roles in groups and use language appropriate to them, including roles of leader, reporter, scribe, mentor

Curriculum links: Citizenship: Choices; Respect for property

Interest words: tickled pink, rock bottom, wend your way, nincompoop, scored a duck

Resources: whiteboard and pens, copy of original story of *Jack and the Beanstalk*, props to perform

Casting: (1) Jack (scene 1–scene 4) (2) Jack (scene 5–end) (3) Mother (4) Giant (5) Buttercup (6) Stallholder

Getting started

- Encourage the children to predict from the title what the play may be about. Do they know this story already?

- Retell the original story and compare characters using p2. Are the characters the same?

- Read p3 together. What do the children notice about language? Introduce the idea of rhyming couplets and ask them to consider the importance of rhythm as they read.

- Demonstrate reading pp3–4 with expression and encourage the children to join in as the audience. Draw attention to question marks and exclamation marks, which tell you how to read the text.

Reading and responding

- Children read through to scene two. Ask them if the voices they are using are appropriate. Think of ways to improve (e.g. speaking clearly, using emphasis) and return to reread scene one. Is it a better reading? How?

- As they read, check for effective phrasing and an even pace to emphasise rhymes. Draw attention to use of italics on p12 for emphasis.

- Read through to the end of the play and discuss use of voice. Think about the way people speak, e.g. mother → shouts, questions, commands.

- Ask the children to skim through the text and find examples of powerful verbs (*sprung, hurtled, broke*), and add these to the whiteboard.